The Apocryphal Gospels: The History Included

By Gustavo Vázquez-Lozano

The first page of the Gospel of Judas

About Charles River Editors

Charles River Editors is a boutique digital publishing company, specializing in bringing history back to life with educational and engaging books on a wide range of topics. Keep up to date with our new and free offerings with this 5 second sign up on our weekly mailing list, and visit Our Kindle Author Page to see other recently published Kindle titles.

We make these books for you and always want to know our readers' opinions, so we encourage you to leave reviews and look forward to publishing new and exciting titles each week.

Introduction

First page of the Gospel of Mark in Armenian, by Sargis Pitsak, 14th century.

The Apocryphal Gospels

The Bible is the most famous book in the world, read by a countless number of Christians and others over the centuries. Even those who aren't Christian or remotely religious can rattle off Matthew, Mark, Luke, and John as the first four gospels of the New Testament, and books like Genesis and Exodus include some of the most famous stories in human history.

Between 50 and 90 CE, the various writings that comprise the New Testament were written, including the Four Gospels, the Acts of the Apostles, the Epistles of Paul, and other letters to more general communities of the early Church. But what is recognized as the 26 books of the New Testament today, in literally hundreds of English translations, actually took several more centuries to be determined as "canonical" by the Church. In fact, it was not until a synod in Rome in 382 that the Church in the West formally adopted a list of the canonical books of the

New Testament.

For the intervening three centuries, there was much discussion among different writers over the many manuscripts circulating among the early Christian communities. Many of the manuscripts were anonymously authored by members of early heretical groups of Christians who shaped supposedly inspired writings to provide support for their doctrinal positions. Many more had the veneer of inspired texts because they were attributed to one of the Twelve Apostles or Mary, the mother of Jesus; they claimed to offer details of Jesus' life not covered in depth in the Four Gospels (such as his infancy and childhood), or the activities of the named apostle, or doctrinal teachings.

Finally, there were writings that put forward mainstream, orthodox Christian teachings of the 1st and 2nd centuries; in some cases they were authored by the successors of the apostles, in others the authors were anonymous. While the writings in the first two categories were never seen as inspired by the early fathers of the church (the first post-apostolic bishops, teachers, and theologians in the first three centuries after Christ), there was dispute among different scholars about the status of these writings as Scripture. In the end, however, these writings were not included in the canon of the New Testament. Instead, they became the first non-biblical writings of the church.

The process of determining the Canon of the New Testament was a long one. It involved numerous scholars directed by the teachings of the Church sifting through numerous manuscripts with various attributed authorships. The 29 that made it into the canon were those that passed muster in terms of apostolic authorship and conformity to orthodox Church teaching. Most of those that did not make it in failed on those two accounts. Others were not included because they were judged not to have been written under the inspiration of the Holy Spirit. Whatever the reason they were excluded, the writings that comprise the New Testament Apocrypha, while not inspired Scripture, do show something of the context in which the early Church developed its doctrines and its writings.

Even today, not every branch of the Christian church agrees on which writings should be regarded as "canonical" and which are "apocryphal", even though some apocryphal texts often have noticeable links with books regarded as "canonical". Regardless, the New Testament Apocrypha refers to texts written by early Christians that were not included in the Bible used by the main branches of Christianity today. These texts vary in subject matter, with some being accounts of Jesus, others being about the nature of God, and still others being accounts and teachings of Jesus' apostles. What makes them fascinating is not just the history behind why they are considered non-canonical, but what they tell us about the early Church and early Christianity. Moreover, they offer insight into what sources were used to write them, and whether they shared the same sources as the texts that comprise the Bible today. Given their historical and religious importance, there is still a fierce debate over the authenticity of many of these texts.

The Apocryphal Gospels: The History of the New Testament Apocrypha Not Included in the Bible looks at some of the famous texts that were kept out of the Bible. Along with pictures of important people, places, and events, you will learn about the apocryphal books like never before.

The Apocryphal Gospels: The History of the New Testament Apocrypha Not Included in the Bible

About Charles River Editors

Introduction

Chapter 1: Gospels on Demand

Chapter 2: The Infancy Gospels

Chapter 3: Gnostic Literature

Chapter 4: Apocryphal Gospels on the Edge of Being Canonical

Chapter 5: Apostolic Apocrypha

Chapter 6: Epistles

Chapter 7: The Apocalypse of Peter

Chapter 8: The Didache and Shepherd of Hermas

Chapter 9: The Real Apocryphal Gospels and Recent Discoveries

Chapter 10: Is the Canon Closed?

A List of the New Testament Apocrypha

Online Resources

Bibliography

English Editions of the Apostolic Fathers

English Editions of the "New Testament Apocrypha"

English Editions of Gnostic Writings

Introductions and Treatises

Free Books by Charles River Editors

Discounted Books by Charles River Editors

Chapter 1: Gospels on Demand

Jesus of Nazareth was a Jewish, peasant preacher who lived in the first third of the first century CE. During a Passover celebration in Jerusalem, he was sentenced to death —by crucifixion specifically— upon the orders of the imperial authority of Rome, which at that time had control of his country.

Many other things could be said about his life, but apart from this short summary and perhaps one or two other details, little else would have all biblical scholars raise their hands in agreement. Part of the debates center over the fact that the literature and viewpoints written during the 250 years after the death of this relatively unknown Jewish preacher was abundant, almost strident. How many people attempted to leave an account of the life and words of Jesus of Nazareth? Just about everyone is familiar with the authors of the Gospels according to Matthew, Mark, Luke and John, the books found in the New Testament, but far fewer know about the other books that were kept out of the Bible for various reasons.[i]

For some it may come as a surprise to learn that the gospels in the Bible are but a very small sample of those that were produced. From the beginning, the literary output of those who considered Jesus as their Messiah was ample. Without considering the brief mentions about his life in the letters of St. Paul during the first two centuries, many other collections of sayings and deeds of the Jewish teacher were authored, some of them probably by eyewitnesses, or at least Christians of the second generation (disciples of Jesus´s disciples).[ii] Some of these texts were so popular and enjoyed so much diffusion that have left their mark to this day. The names of the Magi (Melchior, Gaspar and Balthasar), the tradition that Jesus' father Joseph was a widower, the names of the robbers who perished with him on the cross (Dismas and Gestas), and Pilate´s wife, to name just a few examples, all come from the Apocrypha and thus are never mentioned in the Bible. The stunning painting in the church of San Paolo Maggiore in Naples, showing San Pedro fighting Simon the Magician, also comes from the apocryphal imagery.[iii]

The Gospel of Luke, one of the accounts accepted from the beginning, starts his work acknowledging that "many" had already written what he intended to write: a life of Jesus and the early church. Most scholars date his composition around 80 CE, which means that between the first and second generation of Christians, many other "Lives of Jesus" were in circulation.[iv] Where are those books? Why aren´t they in the Bible? Unfortunately, many of them are lost, some of them since the dawn of Christianity.[v] There are two notable exceptions:

1) There are two gospels that were written even before Luke - Mark and Matthew - although it´s a fact that Luke didn´t know of the latter´s existence. Both are included in the New Testament.

2) There are some fragments of papyrus and codex, many of them no larger than a credit card that may have been written by early Christians of the first century. Sometimes they consist of

only a few sentences with sayings or deeds of Jesus, and in some cases only a word or two. They have come out in archaeological sites or among clandestine antique dealers.

However, there are also dozens of well-known other gospels, such as the famous Gospel of Judas, presented a few years ago by the National Geographic Society. Moreover, there is an abundant collection of brief treatises, written from the second half of the second century onwards, that claim to be authentic Gospels, although they were not accepted by official Christianity. These are known as the apocryphal gospels.[vi]

Fans of conspiracy theories cherish them and claim they were excluded from the Bible because they affected the interests of the Church or because they tell "the truth" about Jesus of Nazareth. There are between 30-40 documents - the Gospel of Philip, the Gospel of Judas, the Gospel of Magdalene and many, many more - that claim to be authentic reports of the teachings of Jesus. They can be purchased at any bookstore in the Spirituality section, even though most are of little historical value. The larger part was composed several decades and even centuries after those found in the New Testament, called the canonical Gospels.[vii] In some cases, they were composed only to satisfy the people's curiosity, as is the case of the Infancy Gospels or the several Acts of the apostles recounting the adventures of Thomas, Philip, James, Paul and his companion Tecla.

The non-canonical New Testament books considered heretical by the early Church are those that have received the most attention today. In a time when many are skeptical of the traditional doctrines of Christianity, these works seem to offer a "fresh" perspective on the teachings of Jesus. Some go so far as to claim that these works reflect the authentic teachings of Jesus and the early Church before they were corrupted. In this view, the canonical New Testament is actually anything but authentic; sayings and teachings attributed to Jesus were given Him later by the Church establishment that had oppressed the true teachings preserved by those the official Church labeled as heretics. This view is buttressed by scholars who in the last 30 years have sought to "rescue" the "historical Jesus" from orthodox Christianity; the most famous example of this is the Jesus Seminar, a group of scholars who met to cast votes on which of the sayings of Jesus recorded in the Gospels were actually spoken by Him and which were added later.

Because the early Church considered these texts heretical, little effort was made to preserve them over the centuries. In most cases the only record of their existence was preserved in the writings of their opponents, the early Church Fathers. Sometimes the Fathers quoted from these writings in order to dispute their teachings; in many cases they only mentioned the title. It was not until 1945, when a treasure trove of early Coptic Christian writings at Nag Hammadi in Egypt was discovered, that many heretical texts were discovered. This significant find contributed greatly to scholars' knowledge of the early centuries of the Church and the controversies and competing groups that challenged orthodox Christianity for dominance. At the same time, it gave those who questioned the authority of traditional Christianity a documentary base to construct an alternate history of the early Church.

That said, among this vast collection of gospels, letters, epistles, and apocalypses that have been preserved, there are a few interesting exceptions too, documents that intrigue scholars, theologians and historians for their possible connection with the most ancient Christian tradition. Although they are fragmentary, they could contain historical facts or even authentic words of Jesus that the authors of the canonical Gospels may have left out. All of them share one characteristic: they were lost and recently re-discovered, sometimes accidentally.[viii]

Chapter 2: The Infancy Gospels

Before discussing the best examples, it´s worth taking a look at the late apocryphal gospels that have captured the readers´ imaginations. A special group is composed of the Infancy Gospels, some of them of respectable antiquity but of no historical value. While many apocryphal gospels were composed to advance a point about Jesus —whether he was fully divine, or he only appeared to be human, or he didn´t really die on the cross, etc.—, the Infancy Gospels were written with only one purpose: to entertain, and to satisfy the people´s curiosity who wondered what the little Jesus did in his early years, before his ministry. With the exception of Luke´s Gospel, which recounts a visit to Jerusalem when Jesus was 12 years old, the canonical books remain silent about what happened to him in his childhood, adolescence and youth.

In many ways, the Infancy Gospels visualized the boy Jesus equal to the adult version: he had the power of life and death in his hands, he performed miracles and enjoyed a remarkable intelligence that left his school teachers astonished. But the child was also a brat that could overshadow Dennis the Menace. The best known and complete "gospel" about his childhood is known as the *Infancy Gospel of Thomas*.[ix] The oldest physical copy is written in the Syrian language and dates from the sixth century, although most experts believe it was composed much earlier, in the mid-second century. However, this proto-gospel was so popular that several copies in at least 13 languages have been recovered, and even some scenes can be found in pictorial art of the Middle Ages. This is a good indicator that the adventures of the *enfant terrible* were well received among the people. However, this same abundance of versions has made more difficult to determine where the gospel appeared originally, in which language it was composed, and which is the older text.

The story begins by identifying his author as "Thomas the Israelite," writing in the first person so "that all the brethren from among the heathen may know the miracles of our Lord Jesus Christ in his infancy, which he did after his birth in our country." After the brief intro, the book describes Jesus at the age of five (perhaps his earlier naughtiness wasn´t worthy of mention) playing with soft clay beside a mountain stream and making pools of water in his hands. As he touched it, the water became clean. Then the child models 12 clay sparrows.

The only problem is that it was a Saturday. Foreshadowing the problems that Jesus will face in adulthood, the story says that "a certain Jew" saw that the child was playing on the rest day and went to his father, Joseph the carpenter. When his dad goes to see Jesus and scolds him for doing things not allowed on Saturday (creating sculptures), the boy artfully claps his hands and cries to the sparrows, "Depart, fly, and remember me now that you are alive." The birds come to life, like Adam made out of clay, and escape. Not happy with that, the child becomes upset with Joseph, who is hinted to be his adoptive father, and asks him not to bother him, with words that might have brought normal kids a spanking: "Do you not know that I am not yours? Do not trouble me!"

A teacher sees promise in the boy and asks his father to let him teach him the letters. Joseph warns him that the child is indomitable and is taking him at his own risk, but the teacher isn´t daunted. The child not only tells all his classmates and teachers that they´re "puny minds," but that he is the Lord and knows the day they were born and the day each of those present will die. On another occasion, Jesus and his friends are playing on the roof of a house and one of them stumbles, falls to the ground, and dies. Everybody flees, except the future messiah, who remains in his place. When the boy´s parents arrive, they blame Jesus for having pushed him. "I didn´t throw him down (...) He was not acting carefully, he leaped off the roof and died," Jesus answers indignantly, and then leaps, stands next to the corpse and cries, "Zeno, get up and tell me, did I throw thee down?" Then his playmate stands up and says no, it was an accident. Everybody "worships" Jesus on the spot.

The gospel relies heavily on the style of the canonical gospels and tries to echo several episodes of John or Luke, but in children´s versions. An interesting aspect is that this protoevangelium mentions Jesus' brothers, especially James, whom Joseph sends to the forest to bring wood for his work as a carpenter. Jesus is walking behind him. When little James is doing his assignment, a snake bites him and the boy begins to die, but Jesus approaches fast, blows on the wound, and immediately his brother is healthy, while the snake slithers away.

The document itself is short; its English version has about 3,300 words. The final episode is a slightly expanded version of the known incident when the twelve year old Jesus is lost during a visit to Jerusalem. His fantastic and whimsical tone makes it almost comical, and a remarkable aspect is the isolated nature of each incident, the lack of a storyline, suggesting that loose episodes circulated for some time, possibly by word of mouth, until someone decided to put them in writing. Scholar Dennis MacDonald believes that the Proto-Gospel of Thomas and others were read as "novels" in the church even in the Middle Ages, but always as a form of entertainment that were never never taken seriously. Its light and popular tone, and lack of theological statements, lends credence to this argument.

Even better known and more influential is the so called *Proto-Gospel of James*, which significantly expands the story of Christmas. It was so popular that more than 150 manuscripts in different languages (Syrian, Ethiopian, Coptic, Old Slavonic, Armenian, Arabic and others) have survived. This proto-gospel is, in fact, the oldest "orthodox" apocryphal preserved in its entirety.[x] Its influence is felt to this day. Some of its stories are taken for good even today, especially among Catholics.

The best known version of this document was produced in the 19th century by Constantin von Tischendorf (the discoverer of Codex Sinaiticus[xi]), who used more than 20 different manuscripts. *The Proto-Gospel of James* is concerned mainly about Mary, the mother of Jesus; it includes an "expanded version" of Christ´s birth, so detailed with physiological aspects that it is on the edge of grossness; the third part tells about the Massacre of the Innocents at the hands of Herod. Its date of composition is problematic, but thanks to mentions in Peter of Alexandria (311), Gregory of Nyssa (394) and Epiphanius de Salamis (403), we can at least say that it is not later than the fourth century; some previous references to episodes that appear in this gospel suggest it could be of greater antiquity, though perhaps in a more primitive version.

Some scholars want to see in this story a defense of Mary´s honor, specifically her virginity. Ronald F. Hock, in his book on the proto-Gospel of James, writes about the purpose of this ancient novel: "Mary's purity is so emphasized that it becomes thematic and thus answers the fundamental question which guides the narrative: why Mary, of all the virgins in Israel, was chosen to be the mother of the son of God. The answer: no one could have been any purer. Thus Anna transforms Mary's bedroom into a sanctuary where she receives no impure food and is amused by the undefiled daughters of the Hebrews. When she turns three years of age, these young women escort her to the temple in Jerusalem where she spends the next nine years in absolute purity and is even fed by the hand of an angel. When, at age twelve, she is made the ward of Joseph, she spends her time spinning thread for the temple with the other virgins from Israel. When she is later suspected of impurity, she passes a test and has her innocence proclaimed by the high priest."

Many elements accepted by the Catholic Church that left their mark in the pictorial art of the Middle Ages seem to originate in this apocryphal work. Also, most representations of Christmas in the Orthodox Church put the newborn Jesus in a cave, something that is not in the New Testament. The name of Mary's parents (Joachim and Anna), the notion that Joseph was a widower and married Mary when she was a child, so they didn´t have marital sex; the story that Joseph had children from a previous marriage (which solves the dilemma of the "brothers" of Jesus); and the preservation of Mary´s virginity *after* the birth, are all notions that come from this book.

If the most extreme wing of Catholicism establishes to this day that Mary was a virgin before childbirth, during childbirth and after childbirth, the proto-Gospel of James explains graphically how this could be possible. When Mary was about to give birth on the road to Bethlehem, Joseph left her in a cave and ran for help. Along the way, he encounters a surreal scene - the birds in the sky are immobile, the waters of rivers aren´t running, the sheep are frozen in the field, and the people who were working are paralyzed like statues. Then he sees a midwife and asks her to go with him. Then the proto-gospel describes the birth of Jesus to guarantee that Mary remained a virgin, in a subtle way first, but perhaps too mundane after that. Joseph narrates firsthand how a woman passing by inserts her finger in her wife's vagina to check that the hymen is still in place. "A great light shone in the cave, so that the eyes could not bear it. And in a little that light gradually decreased, until the infant appeared, and went and took the breast from His mother Mary. And the midwife cried out, and said: This is a great day to me, because I have seen this strange sight. And the midwife went forth out of the cave, and Salome met her. And she said to her: Salome, Salome, I have a strange sight to relate to thee: a virgin has brought forth, a thing which her nature admits not of. Then said Salome: As the Lord my God liveth, unless I thrust in my finger, and search the parts, I will not believe that a virgin has brought forth. And the midwife went in, and said to Mary: Show thyself; for no small controversy has arisen about thee. And Salome put in her finger, and cried out, and said: Woe is me for mine iniquity and mine unbelief, because I have tempted the living God."

Chapter 3: Gnostic Literature

The Infancy Gospels and those about the life of Mary were not taken into the canon, but they were seen as harmless novels. Therefore they survived in multiple versions and manuscripts, though obviously there came a time when they fell in disuse. But through references of the Church Fathers, scholars know of the existence of many other gospels, though beyond a few verses quoted by the same Fathers (usually to attack them), scholars were unaware of their contents.[xii] According to Bart Ehrman, one of the most renowned scholars of Christianity in antiquity, during the first three centuries of Christianity there were bitter textual battles —as can be seen in the existence of many Christian sects, each one with its own literature— among those who understood Jesus's identity and mission in different ways.

The 3rd century theologian Origen of Alexandria wrote, "The Church has four gospels, the heretics have many." This of course, was his point of view. As Ehrman explains, people must understand that the lost gospels were considered to be "genuine" by those who read, copied and kept them in their libraries. Until recently (19th century), Christians and scholars alike only had a few verses of these documents, and in a few cases, nothing about the contents is known. For example, there are only a few quotes of the *Gospel of the Egyptians* and the *Gospel of Matthias* in Clement of Alexandria, another Church Father. "The Gospel of the Egyptians apparently opposed the notion of procreative sex," writes Bart D. Ehrman. "In one passage, a female follower of Jesus, Salome (...) says to Jesus, `Then I have done well in not giving birth,' to which Jesus is said to reply, `Eat of every herb, but do not eat of the one that is bitter.' At an earlier point he is said to have declared, `I have come to undo the works of the female.´ The Gospel according to Matthias may have been an even more mystical affair. At one point Clement (of Alexandria) quotes the intriguing words, `Wonder at the things that are before you, making this the first step to further knowledge.'"

The *Gospel of Philip*, one that has captured the imagination of novelists and filmmakers, seems to say that Jesus loved Mary Magdalene more than any other disciple, but the text that has survived is so damaged that it´s impossible to know the correct reading. The fragment says word by word (the ellipses represent holes in the manuscript): "And the companion of the… Mary Magdalene…. her more than… the disciples… kiss her… on the…" Other than that, the rest is novelists´ imagination and scholars´ speculation.

Moreover, the recently discovered *Gospel of Judas* was supposedly written by the traitor apostle himself, who reveals that he betrayed Jesus at the request of the Messiah. Most of these gospels, some of which are preserved in their complete form, don´t look anything like those in the New Testament, as virtually none resembles a "biography" of Jesus. On the contrary, they are usually made of long, mystical speeches that are typically incomprehensible to the average reader, where the Messiah reveals the secret knowledge to his closest disciples. More than sayings and deeds of Jesus, titles like the *Book of Thomas the Contender, Dialogue of the Saviour*, the *Gospel of Judas,* the *Gospel of Mary Magdalene* and the *Gospel of Philip* often contain extensive monologues and elaborate explanations about the origin of the cosmos and the celestial hierarchies.

There is a reason why this is so. Almost all of them were written by a variety of Christianity known as Gnosticism. As a religion and philosophy, Gnosticism itself flourished alongside Christianity; it´s not easy to say which came first, but both movements influenced each other. To paraphrase John Dominic Crossan, it is unclear whether Gnosticism was a Christian heresy, a Jewish heresy or an original religion that powerfully merged with both.

At the risk of oversimplifying, Gnosticism was the belief that souls are divine sparks imprisoned in imperfect physical bodies, due to the machinations of a lesser and evil god who created the world. The material world and the body are prisons separated from the divine realm from which people must escape through the ascent of various levels, all of which is obtained through secret knowledge. This secret knowledge was supposedly revealed by Jesus to his closest disciples, and it can be found in the Gnostic books, usually deliberately written in cryptic language. For the Gnostics, salvation was obtained through that special knowledge (*gnosis*) reserved for the elect. If Gnosticism was an independent religion, then at some point it "borrowed" the figure of Jesus to put its postulates in the lips of the Jewish rabbi. The narrative is minimal.

The *Gospel of Judas*, for example, includes only a brief narrative of the betrayal of the disciple at the very end of the codex: "Their high priests murmured because [he] had gone into the guest room for his prayer. But some scribes were there watching carefully in order to arrest him during the prayer, for they were afraid of the people, since he was regarded by all as a prophet. They approached Judas and said to him, `What are you doing here? You are Jesus' disciple.´ Judas answered them as they wished. And he received some money and handed him over to them."

Thus concludes the document, 90% of which consists of extremely long monologues about the cosmos. Halfway through the gospel, Jesus takes Judas aside to show him a vision he has reserved for him. "The twelve aeons of the twelve luminaries constitute their father, with six heavens for each aeon, so that there are seventy-two heavens for the seventy-two luminaries, and for each [of them five] firmaments, [for a total of] three hundred sixty [firmaments ...]. The multitude of those immortals is called the cosmos —that is, perdition— by the Father and the seventy two luminaries who are with the Self-Generated and his seventy two aeons. In him the first human appeared with his incorruptible powers. And the aeon that appeared with his generation, the aeon in whom are the cloud of knowledge and the angel, is called El."

Frankly, it's hard to imagine a first-century peasant Jew talking this way, but the Gnostics had no qualms about producing dozens of gospels as needed, with ideas foreign to Judaism such as the idea that the world was created by two evil demigods called Nebro and Saklas.

Besides being tedious, most of these apocryphal gospels deformed Jesus of Nazareth beyond recognition. Compare for example with the oldest gospel we have, the *Gospel of Mark*, written in the early years, which portrays Jesus as a poor carpenter from a practically unknown village, Nazareth; in Mark's account, his character is a very human, itinerant preacher who speaks in parables about the Kingdom of God in *this* Earth, whose miracles consisted basically of healings and at the end is abandoned by his disciples and executed on charges of sedition amidst great desperation.

In some Gnostic documents, Jesus and Christ are two different beings. Jesus is a human and Christ is a divine spirit that departs Jesus´s body at the crucifixion to avoid suffering. According to the *Apocalypse of Peter*, the leader of the apostles has a vision of what really happened at the Golgotha: Christ is floating above the cross laughing because his executioners don´t know he has escaped and is safe. Hence, Jesus, the man, says, "My God, why hast thou forsaken me?" Supposedly it´s Peter who writes: "`What do I see, O Lord? That it is you yourself whom they take, and that you are grasping me? Or who is this one, glad and laughing on the tree? And is it another one whose feet and hands they are striking?´ The Savior said to me, `He whom you saw on the tree, glad and laughing, this is the living Jesus. But this one into whose hands and feet they drive the nails is his fleshly part, which is the substitute being put to shame, the one who came into being in his likeness. But look at him and me.´"

"Who is really the object of this derision?" asks Bart Ehrman (2005), and he answers, "The proto-orthodox, who think that the death of Jesus is the key to salvation. For this author, this is a laughable view. Salvation does not come in the body; it comes by escaping the body." Thus, the divine Christ mocks those who can´t understand the truth; that the body is a prison and only through death the believer returns to heaven. [xiii] Therefore the passion, death and bodily resurrection of Jesus are, according to the Gnostics, a false doctrine.

Ultimately, the Orthodox (who treasured and defended the theology of the gospels that ended with the formation of the canon) had the last laugh. "Through their attacks amid controversy, the proto-orthodox were able to uproot the Gnostics of their congregations, destroying their special scriptures and annihilate his followers," writes Ehrman. "So effective was the destruction that it was not until recent times (with a spectacular archaeological discovery in an old dustbin in Egypt) that we had any clear idea of how significant were the Gnostics in the early centuries of Christianity and how they tried to fight back."

Chapter 4: Apocryphal Gospels on the Edge of Being Canonical

Most biblical scholars are interested in the Gnostic gospels because they allow them to study other varieties of Christianity. Considering the virulence of the attacks the Gnostics suffered, perhaps at some point they threatened to take the largest slice of the pie. But in the same way, biblical scholars also recognize that as a whole they are a poor source of historical information about Jesus. In other words, scholars figure they are not really missing anything new. But is there nothing else to discover except Gnostic Gospels full of cosmic verboseness? Fortunately, the answer is no.

It is known for example that there was a Gospel according to the Hebrews in the early years, written in Aramaic with Hebrew letters, and Ignatius of Antioch (35-108) quotes it in 107. St. Jerome claims to have seen a complete copy in Hebrew in the library of Caesarea and that the Nazarenes referred to it as the original written by Matthew. Jerome even preserves a saying: "In the Hebrew Gospel too we read of the Lord saying to the disciples: And never, said he, rejoice, except when you have looked upon your brother in love."

The Gospel according to the Hebrews also contained an apparition of Jesus to James which is not mentioned in any canonical gospel, although Paul does report it in one of his epistles.[xiv] According to Jerome, the document says that James the brother of Jesus had promised not to eat bread until he could see him risen from the dead. The text says, "The Lord, when he had given the linen cloth unto the servant of the priest, went unto James and appeared to him. Jesus asked for a table and bread. "He took bread and blessed and broke and gave it unto James the Just and said unto him: `My brother, eat thy bread, for the Son of Man is risen from among them that sleep.'" In this same gospel, Epiphanius writes in 403 that the document is in the possession of the Nazoreans: "They have the *Gospel according to Matthew* quite complete, in Hebrew: for this Gospel is certainly still preserved among them as it was first written in Hebrew letters."

This and other gospels that might provide historical information are lost. However, archeology continues to offer surprises, leaving historians at least some hope that they can appear at any time, as has been the case with four gospels that were recently discovered, all accidentally. They are good examples of what a previously unknown document can change - not only everyone's understanding of the early church but also the beliefs of the first generation of Christians, and even of the historical Jesus. The gospels discussed below have generated countless books and controversy, and while some are fragmentary, one of them is in complete form. The existence of a few was reported by the Church fathers, but others were absolute novelties.

The Gospel of Thomas

Martyrdom of St Thomas, by Peter Paul Rubens

In December of 1945, two brothers from Egypt went looking for natural fertilizer on the cliffs bordering the Nile, near the town of Hamra Dom. While they were working, they found an antique jar. Thinking that they could find some money, they broke it and found a collection of 13 leather-bound codices which comprised more than 50 old treaties. Assuming that they had some value, they decided not to report the find but to sell the books individually. As soon as their mother saw them, she burned some of them because she thought they could provoke "adverse effects." The documents began to come gradually to light through an antique dealer although the Egyptian government soon learned of their existence and acted so the documents would stay in the country.

The importance of the finding was demonstrated three years later when the French academic Jean Doresse made an inventory and found several Gnostic Gospels, some of which were only known by name or brief quotations in patristic sources, while others were totally unknown: the *Gospel of Truth*, a *Treaty on the Resurrection* and the *Gospel of Philip*, among others, albeit in a fragmentary state.

The title that attracted more interest undoubtedly was the so-called *Gospel of Thomas*, included in Codex No. 2, a document that nobody had read for over a thousand years.[xv] Of all the treaties in that small Christian library, the *Gospel of Thomas* is the closest in style and spirit to the synoptic gospels.[xvi]

Several factors highlight the importance of this document above the others in the Nag Hammadi collection. First, although some small fragments of the same gospel had been recovered fifty years earlier in another digging in Oxyrhynchus (Egypt), this time it was complete; its most striking feature was that it consisted only of a collection of sayings of Jesus without a narrative framework. For decades scholars had speculated about the existence of proto-gospels comprised solely of "Sayings of the Lord," which would have served as a source for the Synoptics. Some denied the existence of such Saying Collections forthright, even ridiculing the idea. It was not until this text was unearthed that it was possible to confirm the existence of such gender at the dawn of Christianity. The primitive state of these sayings gospels, not developed into a narrative form, could have been, in their original state, the source which the first evangelists used to compose their gospels.

The *Gospel of Thomas* opens with the following words: "These are the secret sayings that the living Jesus spoke and Didymos Judas Thomas recorded," with Thomas being in this case the brother of Jesus. Without further introduction, there are 114 sayings of the Lord, each one starting with the formula, "Jesus said." Many are similar to those of the canonicals, for example, "When you go into any region and walk about in the countryside, when people take you in, eat what they serve you and heal the sick among them," and then "after all, what goes into your mouth will not defile you; rather, it's what comes out of your mouth that will defile you." Both sayings are in the Synoptics but with a different wording and unrelated to each other. Therefore many scholars want to see in Thomas an independent tradition and possibly an older version of the aphorisms, closer to the historical Jesus. *Thomas* also contains other completely new sayings that sound much like Jesus; several biblical scholars, especially those of Jesus Seminar, think they can be traced back to the historical Jesus. [xvii] Some of the most well regarded are:

> Jesus said, "I have cast fire upon the world, and look, I'm guarding it until it blazes."

Jesus said, "Become passers-by."

Jesus said, "Grapes are not harvested from thorns, nor are figs gathered from thistles, for they do not produce fruit. A good man brings forth good from his storehouse; an evil man brings forth evil things from his evil storehouse, which is in his heart, and says evil things. For out of the abundance of the heart he brings forth evil things."

Jesus said, "If two make peace with each other in this one house, they will say to the mountain, 'Move Away,' and it will move away."

Jesus said, "Two will rest on a bed: the one will die, and other will live."

Jesus said, "Why do you wash the outside of the cup? Do you not realize that he who made he inside is the same one who made the outside?"

Jesus said, "The Kingdom of the [Father] is like a certain woman who was carrying a jar full of meal. While she was walking [on] a road, still some distance from home, the handle of the jar broke and the meal emptied out behind her on the road. She did not realize it; she had noticed no accident. When she reached her house, she set the jar down and found it empty."

Jesus said, "The Kingdom of the Father is like a certain man who wanted to kill a powerful man. In his own house he drew his sword and stuck it into the wall in order to find out whether his hand could carry through. Then he slew the powerful man."

Furthermore, these sayings are not ordered in a way that reveals any overall plan of composition. Sometimes, sayings are kept together by a similarity of form or because they share the same catchword. Perhaps most intriguingly, many of the sayings have parallels in the canonical gospels. For example:

20. The disciples said to Jesus, "Tell us what Heaven's kingdom is like."

He said to them, "It's like a mustard seed, the smallest of all seeds, but when it falls on prepared soil, it produces a large plant and becomes a shelter for birds of the sky."

24. His disciples said, "Show us the place where you are, for we must seek it."

He said to them, "Anyone here with two ears had better listen! There is light within a person of light, and it shines on the whole world. If it does not shine, it is dark."

57 Jesus said, "The Father's kingdom is like a person who has [good] seed. His enemy came

during the night and sowed weeds among the good seed. The person did not let the workers pull up the weeds, but said to them, 'No, otherwise you might go to pull up the weeds and pull up the wheat along with them.' For on the day of the harvest the weeds will be conspicuous, and will be pulled up and burned."

65. He said, "A [...] person owned a vineyard and rented it to some farmers, so they could work it and he could collect its crop from them. He sent his slave so the farmers would give him the vineyard's crop. They grabbed him, beat him, and almost killed him, and the slave returned and told his master. His master said, 'Perhaps he didn't know them.' He sent another slave, and the farmers beat that one as well. Then the master sent his son and said, 'Perhaps they'll show my son some respect.' Because the farmers knew that he was the heir to the vineyard, they grabbed him and killed him. Anyone here with two ears had better listen!"

The similarities raise a big question: did the author of *Thomas* know the canonical gospels, copy from them, and later add new material, or is it an independent tradition? Opinions have varied, but the consensus at this point seems to be on the side of the independence of Thomas.

Although some have traced the *original* composition of this sayings collection to the first century, even as early as 50 CE, the aphorisms collection as was discovered at Nag Hammadi shows signs of having been edited, re-elaborated and augmented with other sayings of gnostic flavor, whose authorship could hardly be attributed to Jesus. It has been hotly debated which ones are authentic words of Jesus and which ones betray gnostic interests foreign to Judaism and therefore without historical value. There are some bizarre ones, such as, "If you fast, you will give rise to sin for yourselves; and if you pray, you will be condemned; and if you give alms, you will do harm to your spirits." Another interesting one closes the treatise; in a dialogue between Peter and Jesus; the apostle says, "Let Mary leave us, for women are not worthy of life." Jesus answers, "I myself shall lead her in order to make her male, so that she too may become a living spirit resembling you males. For every woman who will make herself male will enter the Kingdom of Heaven."

In October 1959, 15 years after the discovery of the manuscripts in a cave, an international team of five experts in the Coptic language, Hebrew, early Christianity and Gnosticism published the Gospel of Thomas in England, Holland, France and Germany simultaneously, as an advance for several annotated editions that followed. "This collection of 114 sayings attributed to Jesus is certainly the most important part of the library for understanding the historical Jesus and the beginning of Christianity," said James M. Robinson, the coordinator of the team. "It alone would make the Nag Hammadi library a very important discovery."

What the Gospel of Thomas made clear is that there were indeed Gospels consisting only of sayings of the Lord (thus confirming the hypothesis of a Q document[xviii]), not counting the fact that after its publication in the early 1970s, *Thomas* fueled the discussion on the varieties of early Christianity. "Jesus Seminar members believe Thomas to be a crucial piece of evidence that casts much light on the Jesus of history. Most of them certainly believe Thomas to be very early, and they believe that it contains some of the earliest sayings of Jesus," wrote Yuri Kuchinsky, author of *The Magdalene Gospel: A Journey Behind the New Testament*. To such extent this belief influenced the Jesus Seminar, that the team included the Gospel of Thomas in his annotated edition of the New Testament, along with those of Mark, Matthew, Luke and John.

Perhaps they were a bit carried away by enthusiasm, but it is difficult to reconcile the non-canonical status of the *Gospel of Thomas* with the portions that parallel the canonical gospels. Does *Thomas* represent an example of an anonymous advocate of a heresy borrowing from accepted gospel accounts to give legitimacy to his gospel? Or is it a separate, independent collection of actual sayings of Jesus, most of which did not make it into the accepted accounts? The early Church certainly knew of the *Gospel of Thomas*, and ascribed to it heretical status. Around 233 CE, Origen (who identified as canonical most of the books currently in the New Testament) mentions it among the heterodox gospels. Others who mention the *Gospel of Thomas* as heterodox in orientation included Jerome, Ambrose, and the Venerable Bede. Eusebius in his history of the Church includes a *Gospel of Thomas* in his listing of heretical scriptures, Cyril of Jerusalem also mentions the work, and so does Philip of Side (about 430). It is now known that the gospel was known and used by the Manicheans, who taught a dualism and rejection of goodness of the physical world shared by the Gnostics. From the earliest testimonies of the Church, we can see that there was little dispute among them concerning this book. Whatever its authorship or apparent relationship to the four gospels, none of the early church fathers accepted this book as part of the canon

What of the second possibility that the *Gospel of Thomas* does in fact contain authentic teachings of Jesus? This is a very modern view, and those who accept this view usually do not accept traditional church teachings concerning the inspiration and authorship of the New Testament. In this view, the gospels are compositions of a generation or two removed from the times of Jesus, and rely not only on received traditions within particular "schools" of early Christians but drew on manuscript sources since lost (usually called the Q source). Questions of orthodoxy or heterodoxy do not enter into these scholars' views; therefore the *Gospel of Thomas* is seen as part of this same stream of authorship. In this view, then, the *Gospel of Thomas* seems to have preserved an original form of Jesus's sayings that were later expanded and altered by the authors of the four canonical gospels. Other sayings are independently based on more original forms; this particularly evident in the parables.

The Gospel of Truth

While not as well known today as the *Gospel of Thomas*, there is actually more information available concerning the origins of the *Gospel of Truth*. Irenaeus reported in his work *Against Heresies* that this Gospel was used as Scripture by a group called the Valentineans. The Valentinians, a 2nd century group, got their name from their founder and teacher Valentinus.

Valentinus was a gifted teacher in the middle of the 2nd century who taught a highly developed gnostic system. While his actual writings survive only in fragments, it appears that a core teaching of his divided human beings into three categories—the spiritual, the psychical, and the physical. The spiritual, his own followers, were those who received the special gnosis (knowledge) necessary to return to the divine; the psychical were ordinary Christians who could obtain a lesser degree of salvation; the physical were those who did not believe and were therefore doomed to damnation. In addition, Valentinus taught a highly complex cosmology.

While Irenaeus ascribes a *Gospel of Truth* to this group, he says little about the content of the work except that it differed from the four gospels. A full text of the Gospel was not found until the discovery of the Nag Hammadi library in 1945. Even with the full text, scholars remain divided concerning the relationship between the Nag Hammadi text and the work ascribed to Valentinus. Scholars who dispute a link point out that the text is absent the elaborate speculations associated with the Valentinian system. Some scholars, however, believe that these speculations are not emphasized to make the work more palatable to orthodox Christians. Because of literary and conceptual affinities between the Nag Hammadi text and surviving fragments of the writings of Valentinus, some argue for an authorship by Valentinus himself. While the dating is uncertain, it was composed in the middle of the 2nd century and was clearly composed in Greek in an elaborate rhetorical style, by a consummate literary artist.

The *Gospel of Truth*, while sharing a gnostic outlook, is a much different work that the *Gospel of Thomas*. Unlike the later work, it does not claim to be a gospel like those found in the New Testament. There is no biographical narrative of the deeds, teachings, passion, and resurrection of Jesus. Nor is it a collection of sayings attributed to Jesus. The word "gospel" in this sense refers to "good news", its original sense. In terms of literary style, it is best understood as a homily similar to the *Epistle to the Hebrews*. Like this canonical work, along with other early Christian homilies, the Gospel is a combination of doctrinal exposition and moral exhortation, including a reflection on the significance of the work of Jesus from the Valentinians' theological perspective. Its introduction shows parallels to the prologue to John's Gospel: "The gospel of truth is joy to those who have received from the Father of truth the gift of knowing him by the power of the Logos, who has come from the Pleroma and who is in the thought and the mind of the Father; he it is who is called "the Savior," since that is the name of the work which he must do for the redemption of those who have not known the Father. For the name of the gospel is the manifestation of hope, since that is the discovery of those who seek him, because the All sought him from whom it had come forth. You see, the All had been inside of him, that illimitable, inconceivable one, who is better than every thought."

The Gospel of Peter

Painting of Saint Peter by Peter Paul Rubens, depicting the saint as Pope

The Gospel of Peter was the first apocryphal gospel to be rediscovered. The finding, made by the French Egyptologist Urbain Bouriant in 1886 in the city of Akhmim, Egypt, was rather accidental. The codex was inside the tomb of a monk who had been buried in the 9th century with his precious books, including a fragment of this gospel. The text is incomplete, suggesting that at the time of burial, the gospel itself had already been outlawed by the church authority, destroyed, and the monk was in possession of just a fragmentary version, obviously very appreciated by him. The Gospel was unveiled to the public in 1893 in *A Popular Account of the Newly-recovered Gospel of St. Peter*. So far no complete version has been found.

The story begins at a very advanced point, with Jesus in the midst of his trial and crucifixion. Although the narration is similar to that of the canonicals, this is a shorter version and therefore, some speculate, an older one. There are some revealing details. For example, in 7:2-23 the text says that Jesus' disciples were hiding because some had accused them of wanting to set fire to the temple of Jerusalem. At 4:11 it says that when Jesus was on the cross, the Lord "kept silence, as one feeling no pain."

While certain parts parallel the accounts in the canonical gospels, the author embellishes the account of the resurrection with details concerning the miracles that followed. In addition, the author places full responsibility for the death of Jesus on Herod Antipater and the Jews, exonerating Pontius Pilate in the process:

> 1 But of the Jews no man washed his hands, neither did Herod nor any one of his judges: and whereas they would not 2 wash, Pilate rose up. And then Herod the king commanded that the Lord should be taken into their hands, saying unto them: All that I commanded you to do unto him, do ye

> 25 Then the Jews and the elders and the priests, when they perceived how great evil they had done themselves, began to lament and to say: Woe unto our sins: the judgement and the end of Jerusalem is drawn nigh.

There are traces of the Docetic heresy, particularly in the wording of Jesus' last words: "My Power, my Power, why have you forsaken me?"

Two things make the Gospel of Peter special. The first is that it obviously had a narrative form as another "Life of Jesus." The second and most spectacular feature is that, unlike the Synoptic gospels that shroud the event with a veil of mystery, *Peter* contains an actual description of Jesus's resurrection. "In the night in which the Lord's day dawned, when the soldiers were safeguarding it two by two in every watch, there was a loud voice in heaven; and they saw that the heavens were opened and that two males who had much radiance had come down from there and come near the sepulcher. But that stone which had been thrust against the door, having rolled by itself, went a distance off the side; and the sepulcher opened, and both the young men entered. And so those soldiers, having seen, awakened the centurion and the elders (for they too were present, safeguarding). And while they were relating what they had seen, again they see three males who have come out from the sepulcher, with the two supporting the other one, and a cross following them, and the head of the two reaching unto heaven, but that of the one being led out by a hand by them going beyond the heavens. And they were hearing a voice from the heavens saying, 'Have you made proclamation to the fallen-asleep?' And an obeisance was heard from the cross, 'Yes.'"[xix]

The second major point of interest are its last verses, where the first apparition of the risen Jesus is about to happen. Not in Jerusalem, as in Luke, or the top floor of a house, as in Luke and John, or a mountain as in Matthew, but on the lake in Galilee, to a bunch of disappointed disciples who have returned home to resume their lives as they were like before they met Jesus. This event would make more sense and would explain some discrepancies among the canonical gospels. Unfortunately, the document is truncated precisely here: "Now it was the final day of the Unleavened Bread; and many went out returning to their home since the feast was over. But we twelve disciples of the Lord were weeping and sorrowful; and each one, sorrowful because of what had come to pass, *departed to his home*. But I, Simon Peter, and my brother Andrew, having taken our nets, went off to the sea. And there was with us Levi of Alphaeus whom the Lord ..."

Although interrupted at this point, the story is clear. It was in Galilee, when the disciples thought that everything was over, that they experienced the first appearance of the risen Jesus. Obviously Peter had a prominent role in the event.[xx] Mark ends his Gospel with the disciples fleeing (14:27), and later with women telling the incredulous apostles that they will see him in Galilee, as he had promised, but there is no apparition. Was this the famous lost ending of Mark's Gospel? [xxi] Did the Gospel of Peter preserve the narrative of the first appearance of the risen Jesus? Perhaps the answer will never be known.

As with most of the non-canonical works, the existence of the *Gospel of Peter* was known only from references to it in works by the early Church Fathers. There is a reference to it in Origen's *Commentary on Matthew* (10.17), but he does not quote from the work. Eusebius records the negative opinion of this apocryphal gospel expressed by Bishop Serapion: "[M]ost of it is indeed in accordance with the true teaching of the Savior, but some things are additions to that teaching, which items also we place below for your benefit." Unfortunately, Eusebius did not quote the specific points which the bishop found objectionable; he apparently brought it into connection with 'Docetists'. In another place, Eusebius classifies the *Gospel of Peter* as one of the heretical writings. But aside from these tantalizing mentions, scholars were left with no idea what had raised the ire of the bishop or Eusebius.

The Egerton Gospel

This has been one of the most spectacular discoveries due to its antiquity and the total ignorance there was about its existence, as it wasn't mentioned in any ancient source. The papyri were found in 1935 in a collection that the British Museum had purchased a year earlier from an antique dealer in Egypt. The first thing that caught the scholars' attention was its astonishing antiquity; based on paleographic analysis alone, it was determined that the writing was made around 150 CE, but textual analysis, style and themes suggest an earlier date, which has been estimated between 50 and 100.

The editors immediately realized that this was a completely unknown gospel, and the interest sparked by the discovery was enormous. Today, the so-called *Egerton Gospel* (for the collection where it's included) is the oldest non-canonical fragment found to date. It was published in 1935 under the title *Fragments of an Unknown Gospel*.

Its significance is that, unlike the Gnostics, this gospel could well have been written at the same time as the canonicals, or perhaps even earlier. Its language is not only similar but even less developed, and thus free from exaggeration. Among the theories that have been advanced, one says that *Egerton* was the source of the Gospel of John, taking into consideration the narrative, although the style is more reminiscent of the Synoptics. The original editors of 1935, H. Idris Bell and T. C. Skeat, suggested that the author of this gospel used a primitive version of John's Gospel, before the long monologues of Jesus were added, or alternately that John used the *Egerton* source. In their own words, "as the Synoptists are concerned, we may conclude that (the

Egerton Gospel) appears to represent a quite independent tradition. It is not even certain that its author knew (they synoptic) Gospels at all."

Physically, *Egerton* consists of five pieces of papyrus in a very bad condition. Four fragments were found in the British Museum collection and a fifth appeared in Germany. Today, it's widely believed that it is an unknown gospel without textual dependence based on the canonical gospels. The reconstructed text comprehends 200 lines with arguments with the Pharisees or scribes, the healing of a leper, and a parable of Jesus followed by a miracle at the Jordan River which is not reported in the New Testament. This is the most interesting part of this finding. Sadly, the papyrus is badly damaged precisely at this point, but several reconstructions have been proposed. Here is one suggested by Karl L. Schmidt: "'Why is the seed enclosed in the ground, the abundance buried? Hidden for a short time, it will be immeasurable.' And when they were perplexed at the strange question, Jesus, as he walked, stood on the banks of the River Jordan, and stretching out his right hand, he filled it with seed and sowed it upon the ground. And thereupon he poured sufficient water over it. And looking at the ground before them, the fruit appeared..."

Despite consisting of only five papyrus fragments measuring a few inches (the smallest fragment contains only one letter), *Egerton* has generated vast literature and much discussion among scholars, especially in their attempt to identify what the Gospel is about, what form it had and why it disappeared. Some have related it to the Gospel of Peter, the Gospel of the Hebrews, while others propose that it's a direct capture of the oral tradition. A close reading reveals that the document contained a Passion narrative (in the controversy with the Pharisees, Jesus speaks of "his hour" approaching, i.e., death). Among the skeptics, the opinion is that the author of *Egerton* copied freely from the four canonical gospels and modified them to his tastes or possibly wrote from memory "things he remembered having heard," but this alternative presents more difficulties than it solves. In line with the law of the simplest explanation, it can be said that the *Egerton Gospel* represents an independent tradition, but in the same spirit as the synoptics.

The Secret Gospel of Mark

The last example has been the most controversial among scholars, with the discussions verging on bitterness and even accusations of academic dishonesty. *Secret Mark* is allegedly a second gospel written by the same author of *Mark* of the New Testament, but this one was a "more spiritual" gospel or second edition that he wrote for the more spiritually advanced Christians.

The story of its discovery is as interesting as its contents and the passions it has stirred. On one side are those who think that it's a fraud, in the style of the *Hitler Diaries*, but on the other are those who argue that it's a genuine, unknown gospel that could revolutionize the way people understand ancient Christianity and Jesus himself. Both sides have scholars of undeniable intellectual standing.

How did it come to light? In 1941 a young graduate student traveled to Israel on a study trip funded by the Harvard University Divinity School. Due to the tense political and military situation at the time, the 26 year old Morton Smith stayed in Jerusalem, where he met a leader of the Greek Orthodox Church, who in turn invited him to visit the famous monastery of Mar Saba. Smith was already a brilliant scholar and had published "works of true erudition." When war tensions decreased, Smith returned to Harvard, where he earned a second PhD and became interested in ancient Greek manuscripts. In 1958 he returned to the Mar Saba monastery, which had an extensive library with books of all ages. Not even the monks knew exactly what they had. Smith offered to make a catalogue hoping to find something of interest. Not only did he do the job, but he found one of the most controversial and discussed papers of the century in which he lived, in the field of biblical studies.

In an old volume dating from the 18th century containing the writings of Ignatius of Antioch (c. 35 – c. 108 AD), Smith found that someone had written something on the last blank pages. The unknown scribe had apparently copied in a hurry a lost document from early Christianity, specifically a letter of Clement, one of the Church Fathers who lived in Alexandria in the late 2nd century. The handwritten text began, "From the letters of the most holy Clement, the author of the Stromateis. To Theodore."

Smith photographed the pages to translate them later. What he read left him perplexed. The writing was an epistle of instruction to a certain Theodore explaining to him the errors of a Christian sect known as the Carpocratians.[xxii] In his letter, Clement warned his reader about the misuse the sect was doing of a second gospel that Mark had written for more spiritually advanced Christians. Thus the first edition of *Mark* had been created based on Peter´s memories; then, at the end of his life, Mark had moved to Alexandria where he had composed a second edition of his gospel, with the private teachings of Jesus to his closest disciples. Apparently, the Carpocratians had got their hands on a copy and were misusing it, adding words and interpreting it at their convenience to justify morally questionable practices.

Clement then goes on to quote a fragment of the gospel. Supposedly, this episode came immediately after Mark 10:34, when Jesus and his followers are on their way to Jerusalem. "And they come into Bethany. And a certain woman whose brother had died was there. And, coming, she prostrated herself before Jesus and says to him, 'Son of David, have mercy on me.' But the disciples rebuked her. And Jesus, being angered, went off with her into the garden where the tomb was, and straightway a great cry was heard from the tomb. And going near, Jesus rolled away the stone from the door of the tomb. And straightaway, going in where the youth was, he stretched forth his hand and raised him, seizing his hand. But the youth, looking upon him, loved him and began to beseech him that he might be with him. And going out of the tomb, they came into the house of the youth, for he was rich. And after six days Jesus told him what to do, and in the evening the youth comes to him, wearing a linen cloth over his naked body. And he remained with him that night, for Jesus taught him the mystery of the Kingdom of God."[xxiii]

Smith spent several years studying his discovery and in 1973 published two books, one for the general public and another for scholars, where he explained the details of his finding and reproduced Clement´s letter. Predictably, it caused an uproar. A homosexual Jesus in a secret edition of Mark? The purported letter of Clement attacked precisely this idea, warning Theodore that the phrase "naked body with naked body" was not in the original, but that was Clement´s opinion. According to Smith, Clement was quoting a real passage by Mark and even more, an historical episode, and he had discovered it.

The idea is plagued with difficulties.

- The handwritten letter found by Smith may well be effectively from the eighteenth century, but that doesn´t mean that it´s a reproduction of an authentic epistle by Clement.
- Clement could well be the author of the epistle, but that doesn´t automatically mean that the fragment was really by Mark, Peter's secretary. Other falsifications were written in the apostles´ names and circulated widely in the early days of Christianity.
- Finally, even if Mark himself wrote the story of Jesus and the naked young man, that doesn´t necessarily mean that it was a historical fact, but a creation of the evangelist, like he did in other occasions.[xxiv]

Initially, most scholars judged that the handwriting did come from the 18th century and it indeed reproduced an actual letter of Clement, since the epistle had his style and the use of words corresponded to other known letters of the Church Father. But Smith was an erudite scholar and could well have faked it. The language and style of the alleged gospel also corresponded to Mark´s style and use of words, but Smith, or someone else, could have produced a pastiche using portions of John and Mark.

The discussions became, and remain, heated. John Dominic Crossan, one of the most influential historians of Christianity and biblical scholars of these days, is in favor of its authenticity, and he believes that this is an authentic writing by Mark. Following Smith, Crossan thinks that this was in fact Mark´s original version, and that the controversial passages were later removed by scribes. However, Crossan doesn´t believe that this is a deed of the historical Jesus; he instead thinks it's a description of a ritual among Christians, and that the homoerotic tones are a misinterpretation based on modern cultural norms.

Other competent scholars like Craig Evans and even Arthur Darby —Smith´s own teacher and one of the greatest scholars of early Christianity of the 20th century— considered it a forgery. Morton Smith himself was a homosexual, extremely erudite, and liked to make his colleagues look like fools. [xxv] "Most scholars found his explication unconvincing at best; some were predictably outraged. Smith appeared to love it," writes Bart D. Ehrman. The photographs Smith took at Saba Mar have also been examined by experts in paleography and ancient Greek, but their views haven´t been conclusive; some believe that it´s a modern forgery and others that it comes from a pen of the 18th century. The debate on the authenticity of the *Secret Mark* is still open, although as Bart D. Ehrman notes, "Scholars in increasing numbers have begun to suspect that it is (a forgery)." Morton Smith died in 1991 and is no longer present to defend himself. Before dying, he ordered that his personal papers be destroyed.

Nobody has been able to scientifically analyze the book itself, only the photographs. If the reader is wondering why a chemical analysis of the ink and the book itself has not been ordered, the answer is dramatic - the leaves have disappeared from the library of Mar Saba. The monks decided to cut the leaves from the book and hide them inside another volume. The librarian himself confessed having done so, possibly to avoid the media circus or prevent them from being confiscated by Israeli authorities. According to Bart Ehrman, the monk's words were that he "no longer remembered" where he had put them. "What is certain is that no one has carefully examined the book itself, and it may be that no one ever will," concludes Ehrman.

Chapter 5: Apostolic Apocrypha

One important category of apocrypha contains a mixture of different works all linked together by claims of apostolic origin. Some of these do show linkages with heretical groups, and might be grouped with the heterodox *Gospel of Thomas*. Others are supposedly records of the activities of individual apostles, rejected as authentic records because of the wild stories they often contain. Still others are writings directly attributed to the Apostle Paul, but rejected as inauthentic by the early Church. In all of these cases, these books attributed to apostles were rejected by the Church, not merely because their apostolic authorship could not be verified but because the contents were at variance with church teachings or what was known about the character and activities of the apostles. In these cases, the decision to exclude these works from consideration as part of the canon was made by the Church using standards of inspiration and fidelity to Church teaching as their measure.

Acts of Andrew

Saint Andrew the Apostle, icon by Bulgarian iconographer Yoan from Gabrovo, 19th century

Unlike many of the other works under consideration, there is no single manuscript of the *Acts of Andrew,* an example of an apocryphal work purporting to record the activities of an apostle. But as with the other works, there are early testimonies to its existence. The oldest direct mention of the *Acts of Andrew* is by Eusebius, who considered the work heretical in addition to being absurd and impious. The 4th century Egyptian Coptic Papyrus *Utrecht I* contains a translation of a section from the Acts of Andrew. From the surviving fragments, it appears that the *Acts of Andrew* was probably written in the second half of the 2nd century.

Traditionally, authorship is ascribed to a Leucius Charinus. While almost nothing is known about him, to Leucius is attributed a series of "apostolic romances," fanciful accounts of the activities of several apostles that include their travels and the miracles attributed to them. In addition to the *Acts of Andrew*, Leucius also authored acts of Peter, John, Paul, and Thomas. These received wide circulation, but were rejected as spurious by such authorities as Augustine. They were finally condemned as impious and heretical by the Second Council of Nicaea in 787.

The *Acts of Andrew* is similar to Leucius' other works. The miracles, for example, are highly extravagant. In addition to the usual miracles such as raising the dead, healing the blind, and so forth, he survives being placed amongst fierce animals, calms storms, and defeats armies simply by crossing himself. There is also a great deal of moralizing; one of the most striking passages involves Andrew's rescuing a boy from his incestuous mother:

4 A Christian lad named Sostratus came to Andrew privately and told him: 'My mother cherishes a guilty passion for me: I have repulsed her, and she has gone to the proconsul to throw the guilt on me. I would rather die than expose her.' The officers came to fetch the boy, and Andrew prayed and went with him. The mother accused him. The proconsul bade him defend

himself. He was silent, and so continued, until the proconsul retired to take counsel. The mother began to weep. Andrew said: 'Unhappy woman, that dost not fear to cast thine own guilt on thy son.' She said to the proconsul: 'Ever since my son entertained his wicked wish he has been in constant company with this man.' The proconsul was enraged, ordered the lad to be sewn into the leather bag of parricides and drowned in the river, and Andrew to be imprisoned till his punishment should be devised. Andrew prayed, there was an earthquake, the proconsul fell from his seat, every one was prostrated, and the mother withered up and died. The proconsul fell at Andrew's feet praying for mercy. The earthquake and thunder ceased, and he healed those who had been hurt. The proconsul and his house were baptized.

So much does the text venture into the realm of extreme supernatural events, that, while being crucified, Andrew is still able to give sermons for three days.

The crucifixion of St. Andrew

In spite of the fact that official Church sources rejected them as false or worse, Leucius' works were wildly popular and circulated widely between the 3rd and the 9th centuries, read as far as Africa, Egypt, Palestine, Syria, Armenia, Asia Minor, Greece, Italy, Gaul, and Spain. It was particularly popular among the Manicheans. It was condemned in the *Decretum Gelasianum* (a listing of the canon of scripture with a listing of all apocryphal works to be avoided by

Christians), but survived in the form of revisions and extracts. The work finally vanishes from circulation in the West in the 6th century and from the East in the 9th century.

Acts of Paul

Conversion of St. Paul, **by Michelangelo**

Another apostolic romance ascribed to Leucius, the *Acts of Paul*, was written between 150 and 180 and makes arbitrary use of the canonical Acts and the Pauline Epistles. Unlike the *Acts of Andrew*, many manuscripts have survived. According to Tertullian, Leucius composed the book about 170 with the intent of honoring the Apostle Paul. Although well-intentioned, the author was brought up for trial by his peers and, being convicted of falsifying the facts, was dismissed from his office. But his book, though condemned by ecclesiastical leaders, achieved considerable popularity among the laity.

Some episodes recounted in the text, such as the 'Journeys of Paul and Thecla', exist in a number of Greek manuscripts and in half a dozen ancient versions. In this account Thecla, a noble-born virgin from Iconium and an enthusiastic follower of the Apostle, accompanied Paul on one of his missionary journeys. In addition to preaching, she also administered baptism—an action that scandalized Tertullian and led him to condemn the entire book.

The *Acts of Paul* also contains a physical description of the apostle:

A man small in size, with a bald head and crooked legs; in good health; with eyebrows that met and a rather prominent nose; full of grace, for sometimes he looked like a man and sometimes he looked like an angel.

In another episode, the author elaborates on Paul's rhetorical question: 'What do I gain if, humanly speaking, I fought with the wild beasts at Ephesus?' (I Cor. 15:32). The text contains a thrilling account of the intrepid apostle's experience at Ephesus. In the account, the reader learns that the beast Paul fought was a lion, one that the Apostle had earlier encountered in the countryside around Ephesus, had preached the gospel to, and had baptized. It is not surprising that the outcome of the confrontation in the amphitheater was the miraculous release of the apostle.

Acts of John

Fresco of St. John in St. Peter's Basilica

Another of Leucius' romantic and fantastic narratives of an apostle's missionary activities, the *Acts of John* is set in and around Ephesus and focuses on the activities of the apostle John. It may actually have been written around Ephesus and dates from 150-200 AD. Unlike other of Leucius' spurious works, there is no single extant manuscript. Scholars have been able to reconstruct the text from numerous extensive Latin and Greek excerpts.

In the *Acts of John*, the author purports to be a companion of John and narrates his miracles, sermons, and his death. The sermons reveal Docetic tendencies; for example, Jesus' body is described as spiritual, in keeping with the Docetic teaching that Jesus did not have a material body:

.... Sometimes when I meant to touch him [Jesus], I met with a material and solid body; but at other times when I felt him, his substance was immaterial and incorporeal, as if it did not exist at all ... And I often wished, as I walked with him, to see his footprint, whether it appeared on the ground (for I saw him as it were raised up from the earth), and I never saw it. (§ 93)

Not only was Jesus' body only apparently physical, but the author records that Jesus continually changed his appearance.

87 Those that were present inquired the cause, and were especially perplexed, because

Drusiana had said: The Lord appeared unto me in the tomb in the likeness of John, and in that of a youth… John said (or John bearing it patiently, said):

88 …For when he had chosen Peter and Andrew, which were brethren, he cometh unto me and James my brother, saying: I have need of you, come unto me. And my brother hearing that, said: John, what would this child have that is upon the sea-shore and called us? And I said: What child? And he said to me again: That which beckoneth to us. And I answered: Because of our long watch we have kept at sea, thou seest not aright, my brother James; but seest thou not the man that standeth there, comely and fair and of a cheerful countenance? But he said to me: Him I see not, brother; but let us go forth and we shall see what he would have.

As with Leucius' other works, the *Acts of John* contains its fair share of fantastic stories. For example, there is the lengthy account of the devout Drusiana and her ardent lover Callimachus in a sepulcher (§ 63-86). For a lighter touch the author entertains his readers with the story of the incident of the bedbugs:

60 Now on the first day we arrived at a deserted inn, and when we were at a loss for a bed for John, we saw a droll matter. There was one bedstead lying somewhere there without coverings, whereon we spread the cloaks which we were wearing, and we prayed him to lie down upon it and rest, while the rest of us all slept upon the floor. But he when he lay down was troubled by the bugs, and as they continued to become yet more troublesome to him, when it was now about the middle of the night, in the hearing of us all he said to them: I say unto you, O bugs, behave yourselves, one and all, and leave your abode for this night and remain quiet in one place, and keep your distance from the servants of God. And as we laughed, and went on talking for some time, John addressed himself to sleep; and we, talking low, gave him no disturbance (or, thanks to him we were not disturbed).

61 But when the day was now dawning I arose first, and with me Verus and Andronicus, and we saw at the door of the house which we had taken a great number of bugs standing, and while we wondered at the great sight of them, and all the brethren were roused up because of them, John continued sleeping. And when he was awaked we declared to him what we had seen. And he sat up on the bed and looked at them and said: Since ye have well behaved yourselves in hearkening to my rebuke, come unto your place. And when he had said this, and risen from the bed, the bugs running from the door hasted to the bed and climbed up by the legs thereof and disappeared into the joints. And John said again: This creature hearkened unto the voice of a man, and abode by itself and was quiet and trespassed not; but we which hear the voice and commandments of God disobey and are light-minded: and for how long?

Unlike other works in the Leucian canon, the *Acts of John* is valuable for tracing the development of popular Christianity in the early period after Christ. It provides us with the earliest source concerning the celebration of the Eucharist for the dead (§ 72). Also included is a long hymn (§ 94-96) no doubt used as a liturgical song (with response) in some Johannine communities. Before he goes to die, Jesus gathers his apostles in a circle, and, while holding one another's hands as they circle in a dance around him, he sings a hymn to the Father. Its Johannine origins are evident in its close relationship to the prologue of John's gospel, but with Docetic elements given to the terminology. This evidences a close familiarity with John's teachings and the Johannine community.

Chapter 6: Epistles

Epistle to the Laodiceans

In closing his Epistle to the Colossians St. Paul made the following request to the church at Colossae:

When this epistle has been read among you, have it read also in the church of the Laodiceans; and see that you read the epistle from Laodicea. (Col. 4:16)

This is a rather clear reference to an Epistle written by Paul when he was at Laodicea, an Epistle since lost and not included in the canon of the Pauline Epistles. This reference, however, proved too great a temptation for some unknown author to pen this spurious epistle in Paul's name.

This Epistle has a very strange history. Composed perhaps at the close of the 3rd century, by the 4th century Jerome reports that "some read the *Epistle to the Laodiceans*, but it is rejected by everyone" (*De viris ill.* 5). Comprising only 20 verses, it is composed of a patchwork of phrases and sentences plagiarized from Philippians and other Pauline Epistles. No Greek text has ever been found, but there are more than a hundred Latin manuscripts of the Epistle. There are also versions in Bohemian, English, and Flemish.

In spite of the testimony of Jerome, there were those who accepted the Epistle as a genuine Pauline document, in spite of the fact that it was not included in the accepted canon of the New Testament from the 4th century. Aelfric, a 10th century English monk, stated in a treatise that Paul wrote 15 Epistles, and listed *Laodiceans* after *Philemon* (in keeping with the canonical arrangement of the Pauline Epistles from the longest to shortest). In 1165, John of Salisbury, while acknowledging that universal opinion accepts only 14 Epistles, lists *Laodiceans* as the 15th. *Laodiceans* is included in German Bibles printed prior to Luther's translation and in the first Bohemian bible printed in 1488. It was not, in fact, until the Council of Florence (1439-43) listed only 14 Pauline Epistles in a statement concerning the New Testament canon that *Laodiceans* was officially recognized as spurious; this text is not even mentioned.

Epistle to the Laodiceans

Paul writing his Epistles, portrait from the 17th century

1. Paul, an apostle not of men and not through man, but through Jesus Christ, to the brethren who are in Laodicea: 2. Grace to you and peace from God the Father and the Lord Jesus Christ. 3. I thank Christ in all my prayer that you are steadfast in him and persevering in his works, in

expectation of the promise for the Day of Judgment. 4. And may you not be deceived by the vain talk of some people who tell (you) tales that they may lead you away from the truth of the gospel which is proclaimed by me. 5. And now may God grant that those who come from me for the furtherance of the truth of the gospel (...) may be able to serve and to do good works for the well-being of eternal life. 6. And now my bonds are manifest, which I suffer in Christ, on account of which I am glad and rejoice. 7. This ministers to me unto eternal salvation, which (itself) is effected through your prayers and by the help of the Holy Spirit, whether it be through life or through death. 8. for my life is in Christ and to die is joy (to me). 9. And this will his mercy work in you, that you may have the same love and be of one mind. 10. Therefore, beloved, as you have heard my presence, so hold fast and do in the fear of God, and eternal life will be your portion. 11. For it is God who works in you. 12. And do without hesitation what you do. 13. And for the rest, beloved, rejoice in Christ and beware of those who are out for sordid gain. 14. May all your requests be manifest before God, and be yea steadfast in the mind of Christ. 15. And what is pure, true, proper, just and lovely, do. 16. And what you have heard and received, hold in your heart and peace will be with you. [17. Salute all the brethren with the holy kiss.] 18. The Saints salute you. 19. The grace of the Lord Jesus Christ be with your spirit. 20. And see that this epistle is read to the Colossians and that of the Colossians among you. (Translation from pp. 43-44 v 2. of [Schneemelcher]).

As with the other works examined so far, the authorship of some of these writings is disputed. But there is no question that these writings show the development of Christian doctrine in the first century after Christ. More so than the other works that failed to make their way into the canon, these works have a definite place in the history of the Church.

The First Epistle of Clement

Pope Clement I

One of the earliest Christian documents outside the New Testament, *I Clement* is a letter from the Church in Rome to the Church in Corinth. The author is not identified within the text of the letter. Extensive tradition identifies it as the work of Clement, the 3rd Bishop of Rome and a successor to the Apostle Peter. Little is known about the life of Clement, but Tertullian says Clement was consecrated by Peter in Rome and it is known he was a prominent member of the Roman Church until his election as Pope. A 4th Century tradition has Clement martyred under the Emperor Trajan by being tied to an anchor and thrown into the sea.

As with many of the Pauline Epistles, Clement's letter to Corinth deals with specific questions of church discipline and organization. Evidently, some bishops were deposed by the members of the Church. Because the removal was not due to moral offences, Clement claimed the depositions were unjustified, and he called on the Church to reinstate the bishops and repent of their rebelliousness and their disobedience. In making his argument, Clement asserts that the authority of the bishops derives from their ordination by the apostles, making his an early assertion of the idea of the apostolic succession.

CHAPTER 42 -- THE ORDER OF MINISTERS IN THE CHURCH.

The apostles have preached the Gospel to us from the Lord Jesus Christ; Jesus Christ [has done so] from God. Christ therefore was sent forth by God, and the apostles by Christ. Both these appointments, then, were made in an orderly way, according to the will of God. Having therefore received their orders, and being fully assured by the resurrection of our Lord Jesus Christ, and established in the word of God, with full assurance of the Holy Ghost, they went forth proclaiming that the kingdom of God was at hand. And thus preaching through countries and cities, they appointed the first-fruits [of their labours], having first proved them by the Spirit, to be bishops and deacons of those who should afterwards believe. Nor was this any new thing, since indeed many ages before it was written concerning bishops and deacons. For thus says the Scripture a certain place, "I will appoint their bishops s in righteousness, and their deacons in faith."

Epistle of Barnabas

***Barnabas curing the poor*, by Paolo Veronese,**

One of the continual discussions within the early Church was the relationship between Christians and Jews. Considering its beginnings as a sect within Judaism, the issue began early from the complicity of the leaders of the Temple with the death of Jesus and the first persecutions of the Church. It became even more urgent as gentiles entered the Church and Jewish Christians were expelled from the synagogues. Paul addressed the relationship between Christians and Jews in the Book of Romans, and the issue became even more important after the destruction of the Temple in 70 A.D., which was viewed by many Christians as a judgment on the Jews for the rejection of Jesus as the Messiah.

The continued concern with the question of the relationship between Judaism and Christianity in the early post New Testament period is seen in the *Epistle of Barnabas*. This work is a theological treatise rather than an actual letter to a specific Church (not unlike the *Epistle to the Hebrews* in the New Testament). In the letter, the author addresses two questions: how ought Christians to interpret the Jewish Scriptures? What is the nature of the relationship between Christianity and Judaism?

While the actual author is unknown, he adopted the identity of Barnabas in order to associate himself to Paul. Scholars agree that the most likely place of composition was Alexandria; the author uses the allegorical approach to Scripture favored by the Alexandrian school of theologians and most of the evidence for the document's existence derives from Alexandrian sources. There is no single extant manuscript text; instead the *Epistle* has been reconstructed based on several sources from the Fourth Century and later. The *Epistle* is dated between 70 AD (the destruction of the Temple) and 135 AD (the Bar Kokhba Rebellion).

As did the *Epistle to the Hebrews*, the *Epistle of Barnabas* sets out to prove that the death of Christ on the cross fulfilled a plan set forth in the Old Testament.

Barnabas 2:4

For He hath made manifest to us by all the prophets that He wanteth

neither sacrifices nor whole burnt offerings nor oblations, saying at

one time;

Barnabas 2:5

What to Me is the multitude of your sacrifices, saith the Lord I am

full of whole burnt-offerings, and the fat of lambs and the blood

of bulls and of goats desire not, not though ye should come to be

seen of Me. or who required these things at your hands? Ye shall

continue no more to tread My court. If ye bring fine flour, it is

in vain; incense is an abomination to Me; your new moons and your

Sabbaths I cannot away with.

Barnabas 2:6

These things therefore He annulled, that the new law of our Lord

Jesus Christ, being free from the yoke of constraint, might have its

oblation not made by human hands.

Aside from the theological aspects, the author also included moral prescriptions:

Barnabas 19:5

Thou shalt not doubt whether a thing shall be or not be. *Thou shalt not take the name of the Lord in vain.* Thou shalt love thy neighbor more than thine own soul. Thou shalt not murder a child by abortion, nor again shalt thou kill it when it is born. Thou shalt not withhold thy hand from thy son or daughter, but from their youth thou shalt teach them the fear of God.

Chapter 7: The Apocalypse of Peter

Apocalypse of Peter

The Last Judgment, **by Lochner in the 15th century.**

The *Apocalypse of Peter* falls in the category of works in both the Old and New Testament concerned with eschatological matters—end time, life after death, the condition of the soul in heaven or hell. In this particular instance the *Apocalypse of Peter* is concerned with hell and contains vivid descriptions of the various punishments. The work goes into great detail, including descriptions of different classes of sinners and discussions of the punishment of evil and the salvation of the righteous. In this it also resembles Dante's *Inferno*.

Citations from the early Church Fathers are important for identifying the *Apocalypse* and assessing its significance and influence. For example, there is an early allusion to a verse in 180 by Theophilus of Antioch. Clement of Alexandria quotes chapters 4 and 4 twice in the early 3rd Century. Methodius of Olympus quotes chapter 8, and Marcarius Magnes quotes chapter 4 and 5. Aside from these quotes, we had no complete text until the late 19th century. Excavations in 1886-87 in Akhmim uncovered a Greek parchment containing a fragment of the text in the grave of a Christian monk. At the same time, other portions of a fragment were found with parts of the *Book of Enoch* and *Gospel of Peter*. All were written by the same person (perhaps the entombed monk) in the 8th or 9th Century. Along with the Greek text there is an Ethiopian transition in 1910. This has not helped scholars establish a definitive text of the *Apocalypse*, because the Greek and Ethiopic texts differ from each other frequently.

Dating the *Apocalypse* can be done by using the dating of *4 Esdras*, an Old Testament apocryphal work used in its composition, putting it around 100 AD at the earliest. On the other hand, the quotations by Theophilus would put it about 180 AD. Finally, if there is a relation between the description in the *Apocalypse* of a Jewish Antichrist who persecutes the Christians to the Jewish rebel Bar Kokhba, the year 135 becomes the approximate date of composition. In any event, while historians and scholars cannot definitively date the work, it was clearly composed sometimes in the 2nd Century.

While it is only possible to approximate the date of composition, historians are more certain of the location where it was composed. The *Apocalypse* presumably came into being in Egypt, based on the testimony of Clement of Alexandria. The work contains several references to the Egyptian worship of animals, references that definitely point in the direction of Egypt being the place of authorship. In this connection however we must refer above all to the tradition that Peter spent some time in Egypt, probably Alexandria, and wrote *1 Peter* in this location. Presumably, then, the work was the product of a Petrine community, or at least a group that had some relation to Peter's time in Egypt. Finally, the Ethiopic translation probably began as a Coptic translation, which was then translated into Arabic

In describing heaven and hell, the author of the *Apocalypse of Peter* drew less on Christian sources and more on the Orphic-Pythagorean mystery religions. These were widespread in the Hellenistic world and were based on the descriptions of Hades ascribed to the mythical poet Orpheus. In addition, various motifs used (including the river of fire) go back to ancient Egypt.

With these descriptions, the author combined very Jewish and Christian concepts of the last judgment, the resurrection of the dead, and the destruction of the world by fire, drawn from New Testament sources, as well as Jewish Apocalyptic works (including the the *Book of Enoch*, the *Apocalypse of Zephaniah*, and the *Wisdom of Solomon*).

Here is an excerpt: "But I saw in the fourth heaven according to class - I saw the angels resembling gods, the angels bringing a soul out of the land of the dead. They placed it at the gate of the fourth heaven. And the angels were whipping it. The soul spoke, saying, 'What sin was it that I committed in the world?' The toll-collector who dwells in the fourth heaven replied, saying, 'It was not right to commit all those lawless deeds that are in the world of the dead'. The soul replied, saying, 'Bring witnesses! Let them show you in what body I committed lawless deeds. Do you wish to bring a book to read from?'"

Chapter 8: The Didache and Shepherd of Hermas

Philotheos Bryennios, who re-discovered the Didache

If the *Gospel of Thomas* has received a lot of attention from those inclined to challenge traditional Christian Teaching, the *Didache* ("The Teaching") has received a great deal of scholarly attention from those looking for sources outside the New Testament for the beliefs and practices of the early Church. As a document it is fascinating and perplexing at the same time. Known to the early Church Fathers as "The Teaching of the Twelve Apostles," for over 1,000 years it was known to scholars only through references to it by Athanasius, Eusebius, and Didymus. The full text was finally discovered in 1873 as part of the codex Hierosolymitanus.

In spite of close scholarly attention since that time, historians and church scholars still do not know who wrote it or where. Of all the non-canonical works discussed, the *Didache* is the one we know the least about, and as a document composed from different sources, even dating the document has proven to be a challenge. It seems to have been put into its current form around the beginning of the 1st century, and because the document reflects a very early stage of church organization and practice, it is likely that the original elements were composed sometime around 70 A.D., if not earlier.

The *Didache* is composed of two parts. The first part consists of instructions about the "Two Ways," and appears to have been intended as a basic catechism for those preparing for baptism and church membership. Included are various moral teachings about different issues, particularly important for those gentiles leaving the pagan world. Of particular interest is the earliest recorded instance of a specific prohibition of abortion:

The second commandment of the Teaching: "Do not murder; do not commit adultery"; do not corrupt boys; do not fornicate; "do not steal"; do not practice magic; do not go in for sorcery; do not murder a child by abortion or kill a newborn infant.

The second part is a manual of church order and practice; it consists of instructions concerning food, baptism, fasting, prayer, the Eucharist, and various offices and positions of leadership. Included in this section are the oldest known Eucharistic prayers, evidence of a mode of baptism other than immersion, and a form of the Lord's Prayer close to the form found in the Gospel of Matthew.

The document closes with a brief apocalyptic section that has much in common with the so-called Synoptic Apocalypse (*Mark 13; Matthew 24-25; Luke 24*).

The final work discussed here was probably one of the most popular works produced in the early Church. The *Shepherd of Hermas* was frequently quoted by the early Church Fathers; some went so far as to consider the work for inclusion in the canon of the New Testament.

The book is a religious allegory, in which the title character is led by a shepherd through several scenes designed to teach morality. The work is a call to repentance and a life of strict morality. It is addressed to a Christian community for which the memory of persecution is fresh and who live constantly in the shadow of its return.

Scholars have been unable to resolve questions of the dating and authorship of the Shepherd. The best explanation is that Hermas was a younger contemporary of Clement who wrote sections of the work over a long period of time, finally gathering them together as a single treatise in the middle of the 2nd Century. There are only 3 incomplete Greek texts extant, along with several fragments. The oldest complete manuscript in Latin dates from the 5th Century.

The *Shepherd* is composed of three sections: Visions, Mandates, and Similitudes. The Visions resemble Jewish-Christian apocalyptic literature; unusually for the genre, these visions are do not concern the end times, but the possibility for repentance. The Mandates reflect the form of a typical homily. The Similitudes are parables which are more like allegorical similes than the more familiar parables of the synoptic Gospels.

Chapter 9: The Real Apocryphal Gospels and Recent Discoveries

If the word *apocrypha* means "hidden" or "concealed," then the real apocrypha have always been, ironically, right under everyone's noses. It´s almost universally accepted that all the canonical evangelists —Mark, Matthew, Luke and John— composed their documents using older sources. Luke and Matthew, for example, have identical passages, letter by letter, suggesting that both copied from an older source that scholars have called "Q," from the German word *Quelle* meaning "source." Although the "Q" source has never been found, one can reconstruct it extracting the common verses in these two gospels: "Q" was, like Thomas, a collection of sayings of the Lord without a narrative framework. If the book really existed, its composition must go back to a few years after the crucifixion, around 50.

In the Gospel of Mark, readers can also detect earlier sources, such as the so-called "Little Apocalypse" in Chapter 13, which circulated independently.[xxvi] The Gospel of John seems to have started as a simpler document that consisted of a collection of seven miracles of Jesus, which scholars have dubbed *The Signs Gospel*.

The other real apocryphal gospels, based on the word´s etymology (hidden), would be precisely those that haven´t been discovered yet and remain beneath the sands of Egypt, or in some ancient library like Mar Saba. The existence of unfound gospels is not improbable at all, and there is always the possibility that any day a shepherd from Jordan or a municipal worker from Syria may discover an old manuscript below the rubble or inside a cave. In 2006, for example, the *Gospel of Judas* came to light after being lost for more than 1700 years.

A little earlier, in 1896, two British archaeologists discovered a huge repository of ancient documents near the ancient city of Oxyrhynchus, Egypt. This is considered the most spectacular archaeological discovery of ancient literature. In that year Egypt was under British administration. Bernard Grenfell and Arthur Hunt began digging near Oxyrhynchus, a site that had not attracted much interest from archaeologists. Suddenly, in an old garbage dump, Grenfell and Hunt found such a large library that many compared the find to the legendary Library of Alexandria. In addition to thousands of unimportant papers (edicts, personal correspondence, census, sales notes and inventories), they found works of classical authors such as Sophocles, Euclid, Euripides and Aristophanes, some of them unknown. Their eyes were the first to see new plays of Sophocles for over 2,000 years. The dig also produced several accounts of daily life in the Roman empire.

Among the most eye-catching pages was a collection of Christian treatises, letters and apocalypses that had been lost for centuries and no one had read since the closure of the canon condemned them to heresy. Only a small part of the huge library has been catalogued and edited so far. According to *The New York Times*, of the 500,000 existing fragments, only 5,000 have been studied, about 1%.[xxvii] In 2005, volume 69 was published. That year, new texts of Sophocles, Euripides, Hesiod "and other literary giants of the ancient world" were discovered, provoking great fanfare. No one knows what may appear tomorrow, but at the speed the works are moving - normal for the academic world – it's possible nobody alive today will live to see the completion of the job.

Excavations are constantly carried out properly by expert teams of archaeologists following a precise methodology, and with permission of the governments where the treasures are hidden, and when something interesting comes out, like a gospel, it can take decades for the academy to respond. After that, it will take more years to get to the average reader. In the case of the Dead Sea Scrolls, a constant criticism was the delay in publishing the findings. Regarding the library at Oxyrhynchus, after a hundred years, the cataloging hasn´t finished. A few cases move more quickly, often because the objects - codex, papyri or inscriptions in stone - belong to private collectors.

In this area, one can always be sure that the more spectacular the discovery, the more doubtful the provenance and the academic credentials of the supporters. Genuine discoveries are generally modest, take years to emerge from the academic community, and don´t produce special programs for TV. As mentioned above, the *Gospel of Judas* appeared in 2006, but the codex had been found almost 40 years before, purchased from an antique dealer and passed from hand to hand until the National Geographic Society published the first English translation. For years it was located in a safety deposit box in New York. To make the translation, an impressive restoration process was made; the first step was to set in order more than a thousand fragments about to become dust. In December 2004 a test of carbon 14 was conducted, which dated the papyrus between 220 and 340, while several paleographers agreed that it was indeed a document produced in Egypt between the third and fourth centuries.

Almost a decade later, in 2015, a team of researchers found a fragment of the *Gospel of Mark* in a very unexpected place: inside the mask of an Egyptian mummy. The original document, according to Craig Evans, a respected biblical scholar, was recycled to make the paper mask, a normal procedure for people who didn´t belong to the nobility (the kings could afford metal masks). The team dated the fragment to 90, which makes it the oldest piece of Christian writing ever found, and the only from the first century. Previously, the oldest known document was a fragment from the Gospel of John from 130. Evans' findings will be published in 2017.

The third recent discovery is the most spectacular, but the one to take with a great dose of skepticism. This is a series of 70 metal plates with inscriptions and drawings found in a cave in Jordan, near the Sea of Galilee. If authentic, they were made in Jesus's time. Among them there is a portrait of the Messiah. Currently they are in possession of a man named Hassan Saida. According to locals, the objects were discovered after a flood washed away the mounds where there were small caves, and each had a book inside. The area is known by archaeologists as one of the sites where Jews took refuge after the Roman destruction of Jerusalem in 70 CE.

Archaeologist David Elkington, who has been collecting contributions to make a film, vouches for their authenticity and says they were made by one of the first Christian groups. One plate shows the portrait of a bearded man and what appears to be thorns on his head, which would be the oldest portrait of Jesus ever made (although some have commented it might be a representation of the God sun).[xxviii] Hassan Saida has been offered millions for these objects, but he has rejected every bid so far. However, he hasn´t been opposed to letting the objects be analyzed in England and Switzerland. Initially received as "the major discovery of Christian history," five years after the fact, several scholars have declared that they are fakes.

Chapter 10: Is the Canon Closed?

The current form of the Bible has been unchanged for centuries, but does this mean the canon is definitively closed? Would things change with the discovery of a new gospel, which without a shadow of a doubt is determined to be from the first half of the first century and was written by one of the original Christians of the first or second generation? For example, would things change with the full version of the *Egerton Gospel*, which is known only in small pieces, or some lost text from the very beginning, such as the "Q" document? Would a text written by Jesus himself subsequently be included in the Bible? This dilemma is known as the flexibility of the canon, the debate over whether the four Gospels that make up the New Testament have established a definite collection. In the same vein, could texts currently in the Bible be taken out, like the second epistle of Peter, which is in the canon but is most probably a "forgery."[xxix]

With one or two exceptions, none of the apocryphal gospels - full or fragmentary - has been seriously considered for the New Testament since it was closed in the fourth century. But if it is known that "many" contemporaries of Jesus wrote "a narrative of the things which have been accomplished among us" (Luke 1: 1), the possibility remains that there are one or two unknown gospels still out there hidden away, whether under sands, in a cave, or even in the safe-deposit box of a millionaire collector.

A List of the New Testament Apocrypha

This list includes known and published gospels, as well as lost tractates, some known only through quotes in patristic documents; recently discovered documents; texts in fragmentary state, and one whose authenticity as an ancient document remains in dispute, the *Secret Gospel of Mark.*

Infancy Gospel of James

Infancy Gospel of Thomas

Gospel of Pseudo-Matthew

Birth of Mary and Infancy of the Saviour

Syriac Infancy Gospel

History of Joseph the Carpenter

Life of John the Baptist

The Gospel of the Ebionites

The Gospel of the Hebrews

The Gospel of the Nazarenes

Gospel of Marcion

Gospel of Mani

Gospel of Apelles

Gospel of Bardesanes

Gospel of Basilides

Gospel of Thomas

Gospel of Peter

Gospel of Nicodemus

Pseudo-Cyril of Jerusalem, On the Life and the Passion of Christ

Gospel of Bartholomew

Questions of Bartholomew

Resurrection of Jesus Christ

The Diatessaron

Apocryphon of James

Book of Thomas the Contender

Dialogue of the Saviour

Gospel of Judas

Gospel of Mary Magdalene

Gospel of Philip

Greek Gospel of the Egyptians (distinct from the Coptic Gospel of the Egyptians)

The Sophia of Jesus Christ

Coptic Apocalypse of Paul (distinct from the Apocalypse of Paul)

Gospel of Truth

Gnostic Apocalypse of Peter (distinct from the Apocalypse of Peter)

Pistis Sophia

Second Treatise of the Great Seth

Apocryphon of John (also called the "Secret Gospel of John")

Coptic Gospel of the Egyptians (distinct from the Greek Gospel of the Egyptians)

Trimorphic Protennoia

Books of Jeu

Acts of Andrew

Acts of Barnabas

Acts of John

Acts of the Martyrs

Acts of Paul

Acts of Paul and Thecla

Acts of Peter

Acts of Peter and Andrew

Acts of Peter and Paul

Acts of Peter and the Twelve

Acts of Philip

Acts of Pilate

Acts of Thomas

Acts of Timothy

Acts of Xanthippe, Polyxena, and Rebecca

Epistle of Barnabas

Epistles of Clement

Epistle of the Corinthians to Paul

Epistle of Ignatius to the Smyrnaeans

Epistle of Ignatius to the Trallians

Epistle of Polycarp to the Philippians

Epistle to Diognetus

Epistle to the Laodiceans (an epistle in the name of Paul)

Epistle to Seneca the Younger (an epistle in the name of Paul)

Third Epistle to the Corinthians

Apocalypse of Paul (distinct from the Coptic Apocalypse of Paul)

Apocalypse of Peter (distinct from the Gnostic Apocalypse of Peter)

Apocalypse of Pseudo-Methodius

Apocalypse of Thomas (also called the Revelation of Thomas)

Apocalypse of Stephen (also called the Revelation of Stephen)

First Apocalypse of James (also called the First Revelation of James)

Second Apocalypse of James (also called the Second Revelation of James)

The Shepherd of Hermas

Fate of Mary

The Home Going of Mary

The Falling Asleep of the Mother of God

The Descent of Mary

Apostolic Constitutions

Book of Nepos

Canons of the Apostles

Cave of Treasures

The Didache or "Teaching of the 12 Apostles"

Liturgy of St James

Penitence of Origen

Prayer of Paul

Sentences of Sextus

The Secret Gospel of Mark

The Oxyrhynchus Gospels

The Egerton Gospel

Gospel of Eve

Gospel of the Four Heavenly Realms

Gospel of Matthias

Gospel of Perfection

Gospel of the Seventy

Gospel of Thaddaeus

Gospel of the Twelve

Memoria Apostolorum

Online Resources

Other Christian titles by Charles River Editors

Other apocrypha titles on Amazon

Bibliography

English Editions of the Apostolic Fathers

Alexander Roberts, James Donaldson, and A. C. Coxe, eds., *The Ante-Nicene Fathers: Translations of the Writings of the Fathers down to A.D. 325. Vol. 1. The Apostolic Fathers; Justin Martyr; Irenaeus.* (Edinburgh, 1885; reprinted Grand Rapids: Wm. B. Eerdmans, 1953).

Joseph Barber Lightfoot, *The Apostolic Fathers: comprising the epistles (genuine and spurious) of Clement of Rome, the epistles of S. Ignatius, the epistle of S. Polycarp, the martyrdom of S. Polycarp, the teaching of the Apostles, the epistle of Barnabas, the Shepherd of Hermas, the epistle to Diognetus, the fragments of Papias, the reliques of the elders preserved in Irenæus. Revised texts with short introductions and English translations by the late J. B. Lightfoot; edited and completed by J. R. Harmer.* (London: Macmillan and Co., 1891). A standard edition, frequently reprinted.

Robert M. Grant, ed., *The Apostolic Fathers: A New Translation and Commentary*. 6 vols. (New York: Nelson, 1964-1968).

English Editions of the "New Testament Apocrypha"

Montague Rhodes James, *The Apocryphal New Testament: Being the Apocryphal Gospels, Acts, Epistles, and Apocalypses, with Other Narratives and Fragments Newly Translated*

(Oxford: Clarendon, 1924; reprinted in 1953 with appendixes by J. W. B. Barns; reprinted 1975.)

Wilhelm Schneemelcher, Edgar Hennecke & Robert McLachlan Wilson, eds., *New Testament Apocrypha*. 2 vols. (London: Lutterworth, 1963, 1965. 2nd edition: Cambridge: James Clarke; Louisville: Westminster/John Knox, 1991, 1992).

J.K. Elliott [James Keith], ed., *The Apocryphal New Testament: a Collection of Apocryphal Christian Literature in an English Translation* (Oxford: Clarendon Press; New York: Oxford University Press, 1993).

J.K. Elliott [James Keith], ed., *The Apocryphal Jesus: Legends of the Early Church* (Oxford and New York: Oxford University Press, 1996).

English Editions of Gnostic Writings

Robert M. Grant, *Gnosticism: A Source Book of Heretical Writings from the Early Christian Period* (New York: AMS Press, 1961).

James M. Robinson, ed., *The Nag Hammadi Library in English* (New York: Harper & Row, 1977. 2nd edition with minor additions, 1981. 3rd edition thoroughly revised, 1988).

Introductions and Treatises

Bruce M. Metzger, *The Canon of the New Testament: Its origin, development and significance* (Oxford: Clarendon Press, 1987). This is the standard work on the subject of the canon.

Robert M. Grant, *Gnosticism and Early Christianity* (London, 1959).

Robert M. Grant, *The Apostolic Fathers: An Introduction* (New York: Thomas Nelson & Sons, 1964).

F. F. Bruce, *Jesus and Christian Origins Outside the New Testament* (Grand Rapids: Eerdmans, 1974).

David Syme Russell, *The Method and Message of Jewish Apocalyptic: 200 BC-AD 100* (Philadelphia: Fortress Press, 1964).

Other Sources

Borg, Marcus *et al.* (1999). *The Lost Gospel Q: The Original Sayings of Jesus*. United States of America: Ulysses Press.

Cartlidge, David R. *et al.* (2001). *Art and the Christian Apocrypha*. United States of America: Routledge.

Crossan, John Dominic. (1992). *Four other gospels*. California: Polebridge Press.

De Santos Otero, Aurelio. (1984). *Los evangelios apócrifos*. Madrid: Biblioteca de Autores Cristianos.

Ehrman, Bart D. (2003). *Lost Scriptures: Books that Did Not Make It into the New Testament*. USA: Oxford University Press.

Ehrman, Bart D. (2005). *Lost Christianities: The Battles for Scripture and the Faiths We Never Knew*. USA: Oxford University Press.

Smith, Morton (2014). *Jesus the Magician: A renowned historian reveals how Jesus was viewed by people of his time*. USA: Hampton Roads Publishing.

The Anchor Bible Dictionary. (1992) (vol. I-VI). New York: Doubleday.

Vázquez-Lozano, Gustavo. (2016). *Lo que no me enseñaron en el catecismo.* Aguascalientes: Libros de México.

Free Books by Charles River Editors

We have brand new titles available for free most days of the week. To see which of our titles are currently free, click on this link.

Discounted Books by Charles River Editors

We have titles at a discount price of just 99 cents everyday. To see which of our titles are currently 99 cents, click on this link.

---

[i] They're not a bad starting point, actually. The four canonical gospels, which are quite elaborate stylistically speaking, were written approximately between 65 and 90 AD, very close to Jesus' life. Considering how slow things could move in antiquity, it was very soon. Plutarch wrote his biography of Alexander the Great, one of the most important figures of the ancient world, more than 300 years after the conqueror's death.

[ii] Most scholars agree that during the early years of Christianity, stories about the life of Jesus circulated not in written form but orally, by word of mouth, and it was only years later when some began to put them "on paper." This possibly occurred as the first generations of Christians began to die and/or to set a "correct" understanding of Jesus.

[iii] Simon Magus is an important character in the apocryphal literature, considered the father of all heresies, almost a demon with supernatural powers. In one of the apocryphal books, he fights with Saint Peter in the air, both flying. However, in the New Testament he only appears briefly in Acts as an ordinary man named Simon, who is rebuked by Peter for trying to buy the power to give the Holy Spirit (Acts 8: 9-24).

[iv] Not everyone agrees to classify the Gospels as ancient biography, but they have a definite influence of the genre.

[v] They probably ceased to be copied when more comprehensive versions of Jesus' ministry appeared.

[vi] The word "apocryphal" comes from the Greek language and means "hidden, concealed." In popular culture, it has become equal to books that are not included in the Bible.

[vii] Canonical, i.e., that which fits a rule or canon, a word which in turn derives from the Greek word *kanon*, which means measuring stick.

[viii] Recently recovered means, in this case, the twentieth century or nearby. One of them was discovered in a garbage dump in Egypt, as we will see later.

[ix] Not to be confused with the Gospel of Thomas, which will be discussed below.

[x] In this case, "orthodox" means a document with no different Christology or understanding of

Jesus than the canonicals, as opposed to the Gnostic gospels.

[xi] The oldest known complete version of the New Testament.

[xii] The "Church Fathers" were theologians, bishops and writers of the first centuries of Christianity (after the apostles) who exerted a great influence on the early church through his writings and laid the foundations of the Christian doctrine.

[xiii] In opposition, "orthodox" Christianity states that believers will rise again with their same transformed bodies and will live in a new Earth. As we can see, some Christians today are not far from the Gnostic beliefs.

[xiv] 1 Corinthians 15:7

[xv] Not to be confused with the *Infancy Gospel of Thomas*.

[xvi] Mark, Matthew and Luke.

[xvii] The Jesus Seminar was a group of 150 critical biblical scholars on the historical Jesus. It was founded in 1985 by Robert Funk.

[xix] Raymond Brown´s translation.

[xx] Cfr. Jn 21. Some scholars believe that the appearance of Jesus to Peter at the Sea of Galilee, despite being the last in John´s Gospel, was actually the first one, but for some reason was displaced. Otherwise, how do we explain the presence of the disciples fishing at Galilee, if one chapter before Jesus had commissioned and equipped them with the Holy Spirit?

[xxi] It is the consensus among the scholars that Mark's Gospel ends at 16: 8: "So they (the women) went out and fled from the tomb, for terror and amazement had seized them; and they said nothing to anyone, for they were afraid." The rest is not included in the best and oldest manuscripts.

[xxii] Carpocrates of Alexandria was the leader of a Christian gnostic sect in the first half of the second century.

[xxiii] Translation from the Greek language by Morton Smith.

[xxiv] The choice made by the people between Jesus and Barabbas is considered to be Mark´s creation to explain the destruction of Jerusalem, not a historical fact.

[xxv] Donald Akenson writes in *Saint Saul: A Skeleton Key to the Historical Jesus* that Smith´s was a "nice ironic gay joke at the expense of all the self-important scholars who not only miss the

irony, but believe that this alleged piece of gospel comes to us in the first-known letter of the great Clement of Alexandria."

[xxvi] So Gerd Theissen and others.

[xxvii] See *http://www.nytimes.com/2005/05/30/arts/design/historical-discovery-well-yes-and-no.html?_r=1*

[xxviii] See *Is this the first ever portrait of Jesus? The incredible story of 70 ancient books hidden in a cave for Nearly 2,000 years*. Retrieved on August 6, 2016 of www.dailymail.co.uk/news/article-1372741/Hidden-cave-First-portrait-Jesus-1-70-ancient-books.html

[xxix] Textual analysis reveals that this epistle wasn´t written by the apostle Peter, but at least a hundred years after Jesus' death. It reflects the concerns of the third or fourth generation of Christians.

CPSIA information can be obtained
at www.ICGtesting.com
Printed in the USA
LVHW081112030319
609202LV00034B/573/P

9 781537 606484